Country Home®

The Comforts of Country

MEREDITH® BOOKS
Des Moines

Meredith® Books
Country Home® THE COMFORTS OF COUNTRY
Editor: Molly Culbertson
Project Editor: Debra D. Felton
Art Director: Sue M. Ellibee
Senior Editor: Marsha Jahns
Copy Editor: Mary Helen Schiltz
Indexer: Sharon Novotne O'Keefe
Photographer (front cover): Judy Watts
Production Manager: Douglas Johnston

Vice President and Editorial Director: Elizabeth P. Rice
Executive Editor: Kay Sanders
Art Director: Ernest Shelton
Managing Editor: Christopher Cavanaugh

Vice President, Retail Marketing: Jamie L. Martin
Vice President, Direct Marketing: Timothy Jarrell

Country Home®
Publishing Director: Joseph A. Lagani
Editor-in-Chief: Molly Culbertson
Art Director: Peggy A. Fisher
Managing Editor: Beverly Hawkins

President, Magazine Group: Christopher Little

Meredith Corporation
Chairman of the Executive Committee: E. T. Meredith III
Chairman of the Board and Chief Executive Officer: Jack D. Rehm
President and Chief Operating Officer: William T. Kerr

All of us at Meredith® Books are dedicated to providing you with the information and ideas
you need to decorate your home. We guarantee your satisfaction with this book for as long as you own it.
If you have any questions, comments, or suggestions, please write to us at:

MEREDITH® BOOKS, Decorating Books
Editorial Department, RW 240
1716 Locust St.
Des Moines, IA 50309-3023

Nothing is quite as comfortable or as comforting, I think, as rooms dressed in great country style. Such rooms resonate with the passion we feel for the place we call home. Filled with classic, sturdy furnishings, country rooms invite family and friends to pause and enjoy the space. Because they are filled with the things that we like best, these rooms are highly personal and tell others much about ourselves and about what we most treasure from the past. Country rooms are filled with surprises, too—those collections of things we've acquired over time, like baskets, quilts, toys, garden fixtures, and folk art. And the rooms we call country are both utterly accessible and deeply satisfying.

Like *Country Home*® magazine, **The Comforts of Country** is filled with beautiful photographs of lovely, comfortable rooms, in all the myriad interpretations of country. I hope that this book inspires the best country style in all the rooms in your home.

Molly Culbertson

Editor-in-Chief
Country Home® magazine

Table of Contents

LIVING SPACES

Whether casual or elegant, your primary living space introduces country's richness and diversity. A special section on the Colors of Country follows.

6

GRACIOUS SETTINGS

The dining room is the place to nourish your spirit as well as your body—especially when it's enhanced with treasured antiques.

26

PRIVATE RETREATS

The bedroom wraps you in quiet and comfort, reflecting your innermost dreams. A special section on Quilted Comforts follows.

46

BATH BALMS

The bathroom may be one of the smallest rooms in your house, but it can showcase spectacular country style.

66

COOKS' TOUR

Traditionally known as the heart of the home, the kitchen offers warmth with good food and favorite country treasures.

80

HIDING PLACES

Every home has special places—nooks and crannies and quiet corners—
where you can display country decorating and collectibles.

98

OUTDOOR VIEWS

Extending living space into the great outdoors, the porch invites family
and friends to indulge in long conversations and lazy afternoons.

114

NATURE'S COMFORTS

The garden offers you unlimited freedom to play with colors
and textures. A special section on Decorating with Flowers follows.

132

CHERISHED DISPLAYS

Find three of anything you love, and you have the start of a treasured
collection to display with style and flair throughout the house.

154

HOLIDAY HOMES

As you celebrate the season with family and friends, country collectibles
and other decor capture the spirit of your most honored traditions.

172

INDEX
192

Living Spaces

It's the entrance to the home, the first impression, the warm invitation to sit down and have a cup of coffee or spend an evening with family. The special living spaces in our homes—living rooms, great rooms, and family rooms—reflect an appreciation for our heritage and a love of the learning we gain from the past.

Preceding pages: A newly crafted mission-style sofa and chairs blend with older pieces, such as the carpenter's trunk, which serves as a coffee table, and the primitive bench used for additional seating. Large windows let in lots of light, adding to the airy feeling of the room.

Left: A wreath and garland of silk ivy and roses soften the living room's ornate, mirrored mantel, installed when this carriage house was converted to a home in 1910. Floral chintz and vintage pieces, including a $100 flea-market hutch, create a cheery mood.

Right: Stained-glass windows hang in the doorframe between the dining room and living room. Oriental carpets add pleasing contrast to the primitive pine antiques.

Country elegance can be created with architectural remnants and collections of accessories that make each home unique. The elegance may appear in the wispy lines of a floral arrangement, the muted colors of old stained glass, or the rich wood tones of a mantel that harken to an era of luxury. No matter where you find them, these details add gracious refinements to living rooms.

EASY DRAMA

Right: White and red oak in the living room are indigenous to the area where this 1906 house was built. Geometric lines, including those on the ceiling, are a hallmark of Arts and Crafts design.

Left: Craftsman-style chairs, a handwoven rug, and reproduction accessories catch the sunlight offered by a double row of transom windows.

Below: Leisurely hours spent writing to good friends require a cushioned chair and well-lit desktop.

There's drama in strength—in the bold lines of mission furniture, the confident colors of a comfortable desk chair, or the play of geometric patterns of windowpanes against the sun. Simple yet strong, these elements lead us to special living spaces where we can relax, converse, read, and study while surrounded by the comforts of country.

FLORAL MAGIC

Right: Angling furnishings in this family room's seating area inspires intimate conversations. Details in this new home include the handsome shaping of interior columns, the warm hue of recycled heart-pine floors, and the bright play of colors in the furnishings.

Left: Floral chintzes capture the cheery essence of English country style in this living room, made cozy with sisal rugs and an antique pine coffee table and milking stool. Staffordshire collectibles grace the mantel.

Near left: Reversible linen draperies are folded back for depth in this 1870s fieldstone home.

Far left: This study's neutral upholsteries and glints of gold and brass reflect assured sensibilities. A window wall has been lined with bookcases.

Rooms that rely on a floral theme invite more playful combinations of colors, textures, and patterns. The rooms shown here illustrate the wide range of furnishings and accessories that, when united by florals, naturally work together.

Left: Checkerboard chairs enliven a room planned for conversation and games. Softly mottled walls have the look of leather, while the wool carpeting resembles sisal.

Top right: A passion for blue and white is expressed in this vacation-home living room—an upbeat mix of polka dots, stripes, and checks.

Near right: This basement family room blends Native-American–influenced upholstery, a display-case coffee table, toys, and a large TV.

Far right: This family room was once a garage, but now is home to overstuffed furniture and warm primitives, creating an inviting space for casual gatherings.

Living spaces don't have to be large to be functional. In fact, these rooms prove that smaller groupings can lead to cozier conversations. By capitalizing on a variety of country styles, the rooms enhance the use of the space and the enjoyment of the company.

Left: Brilliant exterior light streams through the dramatic windows, which visually expand the room. The low-profile furnishings anchor the cathedral ceiling.

Right: Natural materials and views of nature complement one another in this living room.

Below: The Point, built by William A. Rockefeller as his primary residence, features this Great Hall, filled with many original furnishings and accessories.

The architectural features of country houses add to their character and appeal. In these rooms, ranging from the mission style of the Arts and Crafts Movement to the turn-of-the-century opulence of a hunting lodge, the dramatic windows catch the light, warming the homes and woodwork with a special glow.

Right: In this living room, tall bookcases offer plenty of reading choices. Floors are antique heart pine.

Below right: This great room is an invigorating blend of the upbeat and the unlikely, from a new chenille slipcover over an old chair to sheets used to cover the table, pillows, wing chair, and ottoman. Refinishing the old brown floor with a decorative paint pattern breathed new life into the space.

Eclectic styles and a playful mix of colors and patterns make these living spaces truly unique. From a shoreside sunroom to a warm and inviting new living room, from a cottage room bursting with blooms to a do-it-yourself great room, each space stands for comfort in its own individual way.

Above left: This sunroom is anchored with ceramic pavers that add texture, color, and solar heat. Bold stripes and summertime accessories brighten the room throughout the long, cold winter months.

Below left: Pieces such as a vintage English kitchen table cut down to coffee-table height and a bookshelf that started out as a Victorian washstand come to life against nature's backdrop.

WESTERN INFLUENCES

Right: Stucco walls, whitewashed pine floors, and cathedral ceilings with split, hand-hewn vigas showcase this living room's Southwestern furnishings.

Left: The eclectic blend in this living room mixes a saddlebag from the Middle East draped across a chair, Mexican masks, Egyptian sofa pillows, and an armoire.

Near left: Native American artifacts and cowboy collectibles express regional style.

Far left: This living room combines English Arts and Crafts chairs, an old Santa Fe candelabra, and an 1880s Chippendale chest in a collection that reaches far beyond New Mexico.

The warmth of the sun shines in these variations on a Southwestern theme. With different regional and period accents, the rooms prove that country style is as unique as the person who brings it to life.

Left: This English cottage has limestone walls that serve as a backdrop to floral chintzes and oriental rugs.

Right: Contemporary folk art and painted reproduction furnishings create a homey mood in this New York loft, which features slipcovered chairs and a whimsical porch swing. The monochromatic color scheme includes a striped pattern on fabrics and a diamond motif on the painted floor.

The pleasures of country decorating know no boundaries—they're at home in the heart of the city as well as in more rural settings. In fact, country style can soften the harshness of city life, as these rooms illustrate. In a Manhattan loft, a porch swing serves as a reminder of days spent drinking lemonade on a veranda. And in a dwelling far from the English countryside, an abundance of floral fabrics simulates the charm of a cozy cottage. Always personal in style, country decorating transports you to your favorite space, no matter where you are.

Style Notes
THE COLORS OF COUNTRY

Left: Blue is quintessentially country, as proven by cobalt glass, mattress ticking, and Flow Blue pottery. Unchallenged as the dominant color in today's country accessories, blue also was one of the most important early American paint colors.

Below: Green's restful promise is attainable in small doses through country accessories. These throw pillows are outfitted in a lush variety of bold and verdant fabrics.

Above: A frequent error in decorating is to discount neutrals as "nothing" colors—fillers that don't accomplish much in their own right. Used judiciously in country design, neutrals can be the most dramatic colors in the scheme.

To be country, a design must relate to the past—and one of the strongest bridges to yesteryear is color. *Country Home®* magazine has updated traditional country colors by studying the hues used in early American homes, then developing a palette to reflect recent research in the direction of color. By linking colors to the past in fresh ways, you can capture today's tastes and the best in American country design. ✳

Left: Freehand-painted stripes and a soft plaid pattern update the sage green of colonial times. Today's palette lightens the early American gray-greens into watery hues, and it offers heartier greens to capture the current movement toward slightly brighter colors.

Below left: Red's impact on mood is intense. To create a stimulating environment, no color works better. Our red palette includes soft earth pigments, bright and true reds, deeper tones, and reds for a soft, country cottage look.

Near left: Yellow cheers and nourishes the spirit like no other color. In American country, yellows are chalky and earthy, including subdued hues of butter, mustard, and brown yellow.

Gracious Settings

Dining areas offer a respite from the hectic pace of our lives, giving us a welcome chance to nourish the spirit as well as the body. Enhanced by the ambience of treasured antiques, these rooms issue sincere invitations for family and friends to linger, turning a simple meal into a feast for the soul.

Preceding pages: A sizable farm table anchors this dining room, which is accented with French Canadian furnishings. The collection of marbled and flower-printed pottery has been purchased on trips to southwestern France.

Right: This dining room is filled with primitive antiques, including a pine table found in an abandoned miner's cabin in Montana and ladder-back chairs from various antiques shops.

Above: **An old blue-based farm table and turn-of-the-century Windsor chairs rest on an old-style canvas floorcloth.**

Above right: **This room's walls, ceiling, and furniture are all painted an earthy red and green with a glaze of umber.**

Much more than a place to enjoy a quick meal, the dining room is a symbol of the things that last—conversation over a piece of pie or a glass of wine, holiday traditions with friends and family, and the sharing of stories from our daily lives. Featuring sturdy tables, comfortable chairs, storage space to display heirloom china or pottery, and an extra chair to pull up for a special guest, the rooms on these pages are testaments to the lasting qualities of classic country.

Opposite: A Welsh dresser offers robust country character with its collection of Quimper (French pottery) and Italian plates. The chairs and pine table are indestructible—perfect for the home's two young boys.

Right: Topiaries in cachepots, roses, and orchard-printed curtains hint at an interest in houseplants and gardening.

Below: Personal style is reflected in the unusual assembly of rare antique Czech rose bowls, Maine pottery, an old pansy glove box, and English cups and saucers.

Far from country's rough paint and primitives, the dining rooms on these pages are fanciful and fine. Filled with treasures from different countries and a variety of ethnic backgrounds, these rooms demonstrate the depth and diversity of country's roots. The exuberant mixes of pattern and color are balanced by cupboards, wall hangings, and hand-painted accents that provide effective focal points. A blend of textures adds interest, too, with the glossy surfaces of hand-painted china played against the soft simplicity of pine.

INFORMAL FAMILY TIME

Right: Glass double doors extend this dining area outdoors and take advantage of a breathtaking view.

Left: Game boards, a set of primitive side chairs, and a tin candelabra brighten this eating area for family and friends.

Below: Antiques provide room dividers in this home. A large cabinet separates the informal eating area from a flight of stairs and offers easy access to storage as well.

Small tables and informal surroundings encourage families to gather for full meals or light snacks at any time of day or night. The dining areas on these pages are perfect for talking of daily plans or lifetime dreams. Or, post-dining, they're perfect for a game of cards or a homework assignment. Designed for shared activity as well as for mealtimes, they bring families together in style.

Left: In this New England saltbox home, which was built from two separate barns, post-and-beam construction allowed the owners to keep the spaces open and airy. A wall of Palladian windows provides an unimpeded view of a valley beyond.

Right: This eating area was formed by removing an exterior wall (located where the baskets now hang) and enclosing a tiny porch. Here, guests enjoy their meals on a 19th-century Missouri walnut table.

Dining areas open to the rest of the house seem to invite guests to sit and stay for supper. In these rooms, hospitable spaces were opened up through remodeling projects or original architectural design. Rough-hewn beams and rows of baskets add interest and pull the eye up, away from horizontal surfaces, for an appreciation of the construction detail and a greater sense of spaciousness. Excellent storage and display areas, too, add to the functionality and charm of these wide-open areas.

Left: A collection of handcrafted antique baskets fills this inviting breakfast area with charm; a southern exposure fills it with sunshine.

Right: This breakfast table inspired a major renovation. Used by the owner's grandparents, it wouldn't fit into the original house. By moving out an exterior wall, the owners made room for it with a larger kitchen and eating area.

Below: A stack of bread plates from the owner's grandmother sits among assorted utensils on the kitchen table. The brick floor is easy to maintain.

Breakfast areas elicit a cheery wake-up through patterns, fabrics, and colors that range from bright and airy to warm and soothing. The breakfast areas shown on these pages incorporate a favorite heirloom table or a treasured collection of baskets or bread plates. By combining the antiques with sprays of bright sunshine and flowers, they start the day on a delightful note.

Southwest Style

Right: The fabric covering the dining table came from Guadalajara, Mexico. The French doors were added during a renovation of this tract house.

Left: Warmed by sunlight, this dining room has a sparse Western elegance. The pottery and furnishings reveal a dedication to diversity in collecting.

Below: An elk head presides over this dining room, which includes an antique pine table and leather Mexican chairs. A hand-carved pine lintel caps the French doors.

The mood of the Southwest is characterized by the colors of sunrise in the mountains and desert, windows that allow natural light to shine, and a sturdy ruggedness that shows in the uneven curve of a hand-thrown pot or the nubby texture of a piece of woven cloth. Sun-drenched and evocative, the style speaks of its heritage among people who view mealtime as a symbol of celebration.

AFFORDABLE ELEGANCE

Elegant, yet filled with country hospitality, these rooms demonstrate

that polish need not be pricey. In fact, they achieve a refined simplicity

by relying on the most affordable decorating tools: strong paint colors,

fabrics, and an eye for the ideal accents. The mix-and-match mood of

the furnishings is elevated to a higher standard through traditional

window treatments, formal arrangements of wall hangings, and table

settings that make any meal a special occasion.

Right: A Duncan Phyfe dining table found at a charity sale is flanked by chairs recycled from a local restaurant and slipcovered in $1-a-yard fabric. A chintz pattern ties the dining room to the living room.

Left: The dining room furniture and tableware are family antiques. The Wedgwood blue walls and pristine white accents echo the exterior colors of the home.

Above right: This room features original raised paneling, wide-plank floors, and a 17th-century pine farm table from Wales.

Below right: Soft-hued stencil designs frame the windows and fireplace in this dining room, which is filled with centuries-old pewter, still lifes, and rustic furnishings.

KEEPING-ROOM HERITAGE

Above left: The beauty of the 19th-century frontier is evident in this dining area. An 1874 butternut table and matching splint chair set, a wood box brimming with logs for a fire, and spare window treatments that let in the light are just a few reasons this cottage has the makings of a relaxing weekend.

Below left: Late-19th-century ladder-back chairs encircle this keeping room's drop-leaf oval table, still bedecked in its early brown paint. The chandelier was made from antique bedposts.

The hearthside tables and spare furnishings of these dining areas speak to the heritage of the keeping room. In colonial times, the room was the center of activity, with a massive fireplace for heating and cooking. In these updated versions, flowers, stencils, and a graceful candelabra soften the straight architectural lines.

SELF-STYLED ROOMS

Right: The book-shelves appear to hold a fishing hat and creel, a gray cat, and books, but it is all a visual joke painted by a friend. The small painted table in the foreground is the handiwork of yet another artist.

Left: Brightened with skylights, this dining area includes a new Maine-made table and flea-market chairs softened with sheet-covered cushions.

Below: The large table in this dining area came from the owner's grand-mother's root cellar. The floorboards still bear the numbers carved into them when they were removed from their original location.

Designed for shared fellowship and fun, dining areas can be the ideal spot to express your personal style through a unique piece of furniture, a bit of history, or the fanciful artwork of a favorite friend. In these rooms, colorful paintings add their own personality to the surroundings. And in a unique testament to history, floorboards bear the mark of moving day in a 1930s home gleaned from other structures throughout New England. ✳

Private Retreats

The bedroom is the ultimate

retreat—a haven for private

reflection, secret dreams, and

personal expression, where

you can create a style that's

truly your own. Here you can

wrap yourself in the quiet of

country, surrounded by the

comfort of quilts and other

treasures or warmed by the

glow of a fire.

Preceding pages: White paint and casual hooked rugs create a light mood for this room, which features a working fireplace and original marble mantel, plus rejuvenated yard-sale finds.

Left: A pair of Morris chairs flanks a 19th-century table, and antique pewter rests on the mantel of this hand-stenciled room.

Right: An authentic wood-and-leather stagecoach trunk, purchased for $5, sits at the foot of the bed.

Below: White-on-white walls, shutters, linens, carpet, and upholstery fabrics create a romantic mood for reproduction furnishings.

The master bedroom is a special retreat—an adults-only haven in which comfort and beauty share equal time. Capitalizing on the luxury of space, each of these master bedrooms achieves success through groupings that define areas for sleeping, reading, and quiet reflection.

Accented by the glow of a fire and collections of personal treasures, the rooms provide softness and privacy to escape the details of the day and relax in quiet splendor.

Left: This guest room features a big iron bed tucked beneath the eaves. Highly textured wood walls are finished with a diluted wash that imitates milk paint.

Right: Old pine and imaginative craftsmanship are married in this Mormon-made bed, which features a bold silhouette and massive turnings.

Near right: This under-eaves bedroom creates a cozy retreat.

Far right: With a chamfered corner post and hand-hewn beams, this guest bedroom has changed little since its historic home was built. Old woven spreads, wreaths, and period furniture (including a rope bed with feather and straw mattresses) fit the restored architecture.

Guest rooms welcome family and friends with a hospitable offering of warmth and privacy. Play up the graceful arch of a bed frame or a cottage door by filling the room with vintage textiles and a touch of lace. The guest quarters on these pages demonstrate that country style can convert the smallest space into a hospitable home away from home.

Above right: With half-timbered, under-the-eaves walls and collections of children's chairs and clothing, this bedroom is especially cozy. A reproduction rope bed is an exact copy of a Georgia antique. Dressing it is a red star quilt from Kentucky. Old rag rugs were stitched together to form the floor covering.

Below right: The cabin dollhouse is old, probably made by a father for his daughter. It sits next to a "hired man's" bed.

When decorated with vintage toys and fabrics, bedrooms stimulate an appreciation of simpler times among today's thoroughly modern kids. Unabashedly nostalgic, the rooms on these pages are touched by whimsy and innocence— childlike qualities that are always in style.

Above left: This four-poster is an antique, as are the hand-decorated blanket chest, side stand, cradle, and pine chest.

Below left: Large windows deviate from a pure colonial style but allow more light in the room. The shutters were built from new wood by an Oregon carpenter who used original tools from the 19th century.

TWICE AS NICE

Right: A rose palette, christening gowns, and gingham add femininity to this room for two.

Left: Bright striped comforters in a boys' room pick up colors from the hand-painted rocking chair.

Below: A country French influence pervades this bedroom, with its Impressionist-inspired sheets and curtains. A handmade quilt graces the bed.

When there are two to a room, there's double the opportunity for expressions of country style. Livened with the colors and patterns that children love, the examples on these pages offer room to share—with room to spare. The smart use of space includes wall decorations that visually lengthen a room, sleeping quarters that stack, a window seat that doubles as a bed, and coordinating fabrics that unite mixed furnishings with a floral flourish.

Left: An antique bed is an ideal showcase for vintage linens. The screen in the corner is a painting of porcelain collectibles.

Right: This bedroom features a lace canopy, lap quilt, and handcrafted pillows. On the antique dower chest at the foot of the bed is a cow weather vane from the family's barn.

Far right: This cabin, now a guest bedroom, once was home to an 1800s mill worker.

Near right: This room's country French wall covering is repeated on the headboard. Antique quilts and quilted pillows reinforce the casual style of the round antique table.

Beyond providing storage and a place to sleep, bedrooms allow your imagination to take flight, creating particular moods or serene settings that harken back to another time. With a nod to history, these rooms build new traditions from the details of the past.

Above right: The leather armchair and fine old desk provide the perfect place to take care of correspondence.

Below right: With its low ceiling and fireplace, this log cabin bedroom is inviting during the crisp nights, both winter and summer, on an island in Michigan's northern reaches.

Set against backdrops of wood and brick, these bedrooms are imbued with natural beauty. The lively hues of Southwestern style provide contrast, and the more restful palette of quilts and comforters accentuates old wood's rustic warmth. With texture and patina built right in, these country styles are naturally simple.

Above left: An over-sized bed and custom-made down comforter provide a focal point for this room, filled with accessories that recall a hunter's cozy retreat.

Below left: Unusual regional finds give this guest bedroom character. The room is richly patterned with Native American textiles, an antique hooked rug above the bed, and an African painting.

FULL OF SURPRISES

Right: Life imitates art in this master bedroom. Soft-hued rugs and vintage fabrics create a tranquil atmosphere, and lace curtains allow the morning light to filter through the windows.

Left: The faux-grained pine dresser displays a collection of antique Santas. A 1920s quilt covers the turn-of-the-century bed.

Near left: Toile wallpaper and an Aubusson-inspired rug imply a fondness for French style.

Far left: A pencil-post reproduction bed enhances the feel of this room's barn-style architecture, which includes a mossed and stenciled stone floor in a cheery gardenlike setting. Painted Pennsylvania German motifs decorate the trunk at the foot of the bed.

Out of the way from the main traffic of the home, bedrooms can be the purest expression of your personal style, where you can take risks, mix diverse elements, and create a potluck of patterns and colors to make waking up a pure joy. The rooms on these pages succeed in setting individual styles through innovative combinations of form and function.

SWEET DREAMS

Right: This room bespeaks serenity with its calm colors and thoughtfully chosen accessories: a circa-1850 coverlet, a sampler signed and dated in 1842, a new folk-art crow, and a trio of sheep from the 1920s.

Left: The afternoon sun makes this pink room glow. It features an antique needle-point displayed on the wall, plus furnishings and accessories found at local antiques shops and stores.

Below: This master bedroom is a study in romance with antique linens and bedding. Vintage pieces of lace have been framed and artfully arranged.

What better place for romance than the bedroom, where a flounce of fabric or a bit of lace can soften and set a quiet mood. This is the place to enjoy breakfast in bed, share late-night talks, and savor early-morning sunshine, warmed by country style. In these rooms, color and fabric sweeten the setting, and antique accessories add a personal touch.

Style Notes
QUILTED COMFORTS

Vintage quilts represent the qualities of country decorating that never go out of style: fresh color combinations, painstaking craftsmanship, and a belief that household items can brighten the home as well as serve a need. As a result, quilts truly are functional works of art, deserving places of honor throughout the home. Often softened and slightly rumpled from years of washings, they add character to any space, telling stories of everyday artisans who believed that all those stitches were just a part of daily life. ✳

Above left: Red and white doll quilts like these were common around 1900. Making them served as excellent practice for girls learning the art of needlework.

Above right: United by color, these vintage quilts and embroidered pillows mix easily with a bold contemporary stripe.

Right: Crazy quilts, like the century-old example in this home's entry, traditionally include a mix of colors and fabrics, such as shiny organdy and plush velveteen. Though they may look haphazardly made, the quilts require considerable artistic skill, as they're crafted without a pattern.

Left: A Lone Star quilt makes a dramatic cover for an antique dining table. Such strikingly bold colors and patterns lend a contemporary look to a home, even though the design is rooted in the history of American quilting.

Below, near left: A quilt made from tea-dyed fabrics has a soft, muted patina that echoes the wood in an antique cupboard. By dipping fabric in tea for about 30 seconds, then washing it out, quilters can "age" the cloth before they begin cutting their pieces.

Below: A wooden bowl gives a sense of scale to this colorful assortment of doll quilts. Crib-size quilts have been made in this country since colonial days, but tinier doll quilts began to appear in the mid-1800s.

Bath Balms

Bathrooms are hardworking spaces, yet they can showcase great country style. Generally small, and often imbued with the personality of odd nooks and crannies, they pose a pleasant decorating challenge, asking to be transformed from functional spaces into rooms that mirror your personal tastes.

ARTFUL DETAILS

Whatever the size or floor plan of a bathroom, it can convey terrific personality through attention to detail. In these rooms, an eye for the unusual and for special colors and patterns adds artistry and interest.

Preceding pages: Raised on a 6-inch platform and placed in the glow of the windows, the tub has a museumlike setting. Vinyl flooring offers contemporary convenience, but the pattern echoes an earlier time. A brass quilt rack serves as a towel stand.

Opposite: A claw-foot tub fills a niche in the master bath.

Above left: Based on furniture identified in a book on Shaker style, this sink vanity is made from cherry wood. The angles of the shower enclosure and whirlpool give a greater sense of space.

Below left: The soft, elegant wallpaper border in this bathroom is repeated from the master bedroom.

A NEW SLANT

By accentuating the angles of their homes' architectural design, these baths give a new slant to country decorating. Tucked into small spaces, they play up the rooms to their best advantage. The florals create a seamless pattern that's cozy and warm, while the barn siding and tile border separate the walls and ceiling and emphasize the angles.

Right: The Waverly florals introduced in an adjoining bedroom are repeated in this bathroom's wallpaper and fabrics.

Left: This crisp bathroom features nickel faucets and towel bars from Europe, black-and-white tiles, a hand-painted sink, and a marble countertop. The walls are built from old unfinished barn siding that has simply been cleaned with a wire brush and vacuum.

Left: A copper tub was refitted to the plumbing during a major renovation.

Right: A mirror and sconces, a hand-dyed hooked rug, and a hand-painted vanity with silk petticoat imbue this bath with feminine style.

Below: A medicine cabinet painted blue and covered with a small flower design brightens this bath. Favorite trinkets— wooden flowers and a birdhouse—add to the room's cheery disposition.

Bathrooms may be functional, but they still can be fun, reflecting a theme you've set for that room alone, or carrying out a style that you've used throughout your house. Each of the bathrooms shown here sets a specific mood through the use of accessories. By introducing unexpected decorating elements, such as favorite collectibles, lively folk art, or bold colors and patterns, you can fill your bath with plenty of personality.

THE WARMTH OF WOOD

Right: Heavy oak trim adds density typical of the Arts and Crafts style. The recessed vanity cabinets have been stenciled with boxes and lines for stylistic emphasis.

Left: This master bath features a commode fitted with a sink and fixtures. The wooden shutters were found in the old farmhouse.

Below: The legs on this taller-than-usual vanity are an unexpected design detail that give it the look of real furniture.

Bathrooms needn't be all cold tile and porcelain. By introducing wood throughout the bath—in vanities, cabinetry, mirror frames, and other fixtures—you can add the suggestion of furnishings with their warm and welcome patina.

Right: Fine oak and marble set this turn-of-the-century bathroom aglow. Part of a stone cottage built more than 130 years ago, the bathroom was redone during a restoration project.

CLOSE QUARTERS

Above left: **A swiveling bookcase makes a convenient, space-saving stand for toiletries. The bookcase reflects the angular simplicity of Arts and Crafts.**

Above right: **A log doorway in a Colorado cabin leads to a vanity table in a tiny alcove.**

How do you turn a small space into a functional bath? Through a combination of innovation and imagination. In these baths, a vanity table just fits into a narrow nook, a bookcase adds valuable storage, and an efficient floor plan of fixtures makes smart use of space in a house built long before indoor plumbing was common. The creative approach pays off in each case, making the rooms more user-friendly and giving them an individual flair.

PAMPERED TREATMENT

Right: Setting a 539-pound cast-iron tub in place required pioneer spirit and strong backs.

Left: This pedestal sink, with its classic lines, is an appropriate choice for a Mediterranean style. Faucets are a mix of brass and chrome.

Below: An antique pie safe becomes a stylish cupboard for the storage of towels and toiletries.

When it comes time to relax, primp, and pamper, a bathroom's beauty comes into play. A primitive American bath combines the rustic old with the stylish new, while a Mediterranean room takes its cue from the sun-drenched homes of Spain and Italy. Though they reflect dramatically different styles, these bathrooms are transformed into quiet retreats through playful color palettes and much-welcomed niceties. ✴

Cooks' Tour

In no other room is the comfort of country so apparent as the kitchen, where favorite aromas and familiar surroundings convey instant warmth. On these pages, you'll find dozens of ideas for country kitchens, all designed to enhance the beauty and functionality of the room that serves as the heart of the home.

INGREDIENTS FOR SUCCESS

Preceding pages: Charming cabinets, a new backsplash, an old stove, and whimsical accessories set this kitchen's country tone.

Left: This island cooking center features a range with downdraft venting and spacious storage areas for dishes, linens, towels, and pots and pans. Within easy reach are drawers for spices and cooking utensils, and the dishwasher and refrigerator are just a step or two away.

Top right: The floor of this Colorado cabin kitchen is knotty, soft pine. A salvaged hardwood cabinet is used as an island.

Bottom right and *far right:* A jelly cupboard and potting area warm up a remodeled kitchen, making practical use of extra space.

The desire for ease of cooking and cleanup was paramount in designing these kitchens, which incorporate modern appliances and open floor space with such country elements as pine and hanging baskets. The cooking islands make room for more hands in the kitchen; a separate pantry offers elbowroom for special projects and storage.

A PINCH OF SPICE

Right: Undercounter freezer and refrigerator units make for a fully equipped, yet compact, kitchen. The cast-iron wood stove helps heat this cabin and cooks meals on wintry nights.

Left: Behind a white, apron-fronted kitchen sink, potted herbs thrive.

Below: An old department store counter was transformed into an island cook surface and outfitted with a stove and marble inserts. The artist-owner created a mural effect, painting tree-shaded scenes within each of the side panels.

Imagination adds interest to these kitchens in many ways. From the contrast of modern appliances against a Lincoln-log backdrop to the folk-art flavor of a hand-painted counter or a grouping of potted herbs, these kitchens illustrate that country decorating, like country cooking, is enhanced by a pinch of experimentation and individual taste.

Left: Old, arching shutters lend an earthy texture to this Louisiana home.

Right: The cabinetry in this kitchen is made of 250-year-old pine. The countertop's splattered appearance comes from a rare Bahia blue granite from Italy.

Near right: French pottery and a host of copper cookware give this remodeled kitchen a French Canadian air. In the corner is an emerald green bin from Canada that was once used to store rice, sugar, and coffee.

Far right: A rugged English farm table is this kitchen's centerpiece. The cabinets have been refitted with brass hardware, and butcher block countertops and recessed lighting bring the room to life. Mexican paver tiles cover the floor, and the walls are dressed with decorative tiles and printed paper.

Old-world style and modern convenience combine in these kitchens, inspired by other countries. Nuances of Normandy gleam in a row of copper pans, while graceful European arches soften a Southern home. Reflected in the selection of color, materials, and cooking utensils, the influences of other cultures add gusto to these country kitchens.

Instant Access

Right: A 1950s kitchen takes on a 1920s look, featuring cabinets that were crafted to blend with the style of a beloved turn-of-the-century Hoosier baking cupboard.

Left: A cooktop island serves as a partition between kitchen and family room, allowing traffic to flow freely around it.

Below: Entertaining is easy in this open kitchen, created by ripping out a wall between the dining room and kitchen.

In kitchens that open onto other rooms, counters and cabinets take on added importance as design elements, and the floor plan impacts the adjoining space. On these pages, the kitchens make use of building materials that complement the style of the home, while handy islands expand storage, provide convenient work space, and define room-to-room traffic patterns.

A WELCOME ATTITUDE

Right: Using distressed pine on the fronts of appliances contributes to this kitchen's French country style. A showplace for international cooking implements, the kitchen features Turkish and French copper, Dutch saltware crocks and jugs, and blue-and-white export porcelains displayed on special perches.

Light and airy kitchens set the tone for the rest of the home—particularly when they're the first stop through the back door or the handiest place to pull up a chair and chat. These kitchens lend personality to their homes via their feeling of spaciousness, and through the welcome they extend to family and friends alike.

Left: Small but carefully designed, this kitchen is perfect for entertaining. Painted wood cabinets and a knotty pine ceiling blend the summer-camp look with state-of-the-art appliances.

Above right: With a floor plan that is ideal for entertaining, this kitchen is enhanced by congenial colors, textures, and patterns that are Scandinavian in origin. The chairs are carved from the trunk of a basswood tree.

Below right: To accommodate a family in which everyone cooks, this kitchen has two work areas, including an extra sink and oven. The additional work space and streamlined appearance are ideal for this seaside home, where a casual attitude is the key.

NATURAL SURROUNDINGS

Right: In this small and easygoing island cottage, the kitchen occupies a third of the main floor, which is one open room. To economize in finishing the home, the owners used pine for the floors and poplar for the kitchen counter. Delft blue kitchen window tiles from Holland illustrate the home-owners' appreciation of their roots.

The kitchens on these pages take their cues from the lifestyles represented by each of the houses. In a streamlined island cottage, the kitchen plays a starring role as part of the main floor, where it is artfully blended into the home's architectural design. A seaside house, both simple and spacious, makes room for a vacationing family that loves to cook. And a home where entertaining is a frequent event shows off the family's Scandinavian heritage for guests to enjoy.

COUNTRY CONVENIENCE

Left: This semicircular snack table has a tile surface that matches other countertops. The brightly painted, grooved wooden paneling and pale blue bead-board ceilings lend old-fashioned cottage charm.

Right: Efficient use of space allows for the latest appliances and handsome cabinetry in a tiny kitchen.

Below: Used as a guesthouse, an old barn includes this well-stocked kitchen. The blue-and-white colors of the table and chairs reflect a Scandinavian heritage.

These kitchens made the most of small spaces by packing seating and preparation room into compact arrangements. With individual characteristics, such as a bold red sink (a reminder of a kitchen's past life as a school bus barn), old-fashioned grooved paneling, or soft Scandinavian colors, these country kitchens combine personality with convenience.

Left: Tiles from a local turn-of-the-century shop line this kitchen floor. The dish-washer's hand-painted mural reflects the new home's colonial spirit.

Right: Wall cabinets were banished in favor of open display space and bookshelves. A collection of pre-World War II Fiestaware brightens the hutch.

Below: The kitchen in this 1810 Federal-style farmhouse was ex-panded into a breeze-way. Arched French doors afford a view of the garden. Marble counters top twin islands—one offers seating and the other has a warming oven and sink.

Through processes of remodeling, thoughtful design, and expansion, the kitchens on these pages capitalize on a pleasing combination of form and function. Space has been maximized for seating or extra preparation room, furnishings fit the size and style of their surroundings, and a casual eating area now provides a front-row view of the chef's efforts. ✳

Hiding Places

Every home has special places—the silent corners and tucked-away spaces that can be emphasized with a splash of color, an artful arrangement, or a treasured antique. No matter what the style, size, or age of your home, these pages will help you find your niche.

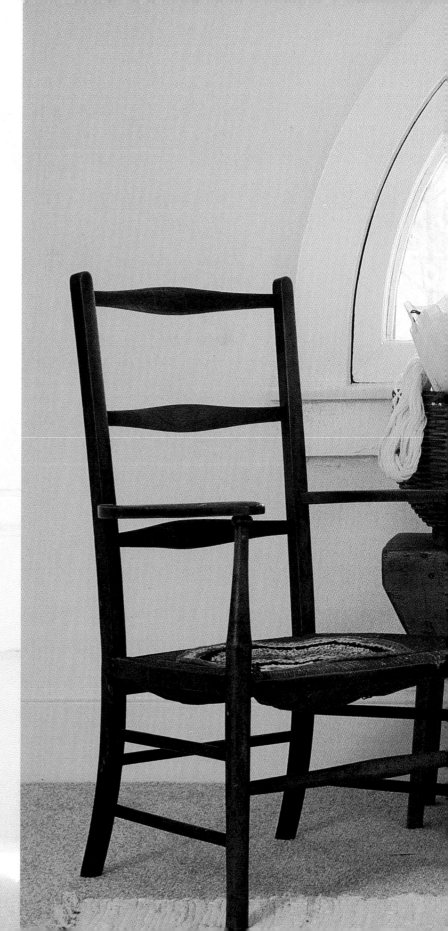

SIMPLE SHOWCASES

Displaying crafts and collectibles is simple in a country house, where a little imagination can turn an ordinary corner or flight of stairs into a backdrop for family treasures. The fireplace mantel, steps, and built-in shelves on these pages show off a variety of collections with inspirational style.

Preceding pages: A builder renovated this third-floor space by replacing deteriorating plaster and adding paint and carpet. The half-moon window is on the front side of the house.

Opposite: An original built-in cupboard houses an extensive yellowware collection.

Above left: Hand-carved duck decoys hang from a keeping-room mantel.

Left: A step-by-step view of dolls, stuffed animals, and other items hand-crafted by the owner reveals the diversity of the collection.

Left: A pillow-strewn sleigh bed and plump wing chair invite laid-back moments of leisure.

Right: This keeping room combines a kitchen work area with comfortable seating space. Filled with blue-and-white enamelware, the room is dominated by an old table with a two-board top and tapered legs. Between two upholstered chairs stands a Virginia chest decorated in its original sponge paint.

Below: Muted, tea-stained colors in a gardener's library bring warmth to this corner.

You can create a niche in any room of the house. Simply look around for the most likely location, whether it's in a family room, den, or kitchen, then define a space for quiet conversation or keeping company with a good book. The rooms on these pages turn plain corners into special spaces by combining comfortable seating with splashes of color, warm lighting, and items that create interest on shelves and as wall groupings.

Left: A long, low bench provides display space even in a narrow hall. The clothing above the bench dates from the mid-1800s.

Top right: A sitting room and bedroom are joined by a short hallway, which defines space with the use of bold floor tiles.

Near right: Original hues still brighten this rattail-hinged armoire from Canada.

Far right: This hallway is embellished with early-19th-century stencil designs, hand-painted when the house was recently refurbished.

Combining utility and imagination, these hallways make "just passing through" a distinct pleasure. The intimate spaces allow unique arrangements of furniture or collectibles, offering endless decorating possibilities when treated as another room in the house.

Desk Set

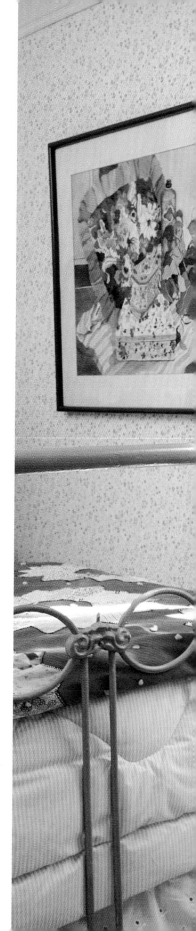

Placed in a pretty spot of its own, a desk sets the scene for quiet concentration or contemplation—ideal for homework, correspondence, or even a sunlit summer breakfast. The rooms on these pages create spaces for mental retreat through simple but effective arrangement of furniture. Positioned next to a window seat, a desk becomes part of a small grouping; set by a window, it joins with the great outdoors.

Right: This girl's room is filled with whimsy. The wicker writing table is outfitted with a tea tray and crowned with a hat and dried flowers. Simple bows tied in the center give the curtains a distinctively soft yet simple look.

Left: A yard-sale desk becomes funtional art with a trompe l'oeil blotter and decorative panel trim hand-painted by the owner.

ABOVE AND BELOW

Look high and low to find extra spaces for storage and display. On these pages, a beam is home to a collection of miniatures, an under-stairs alcove makes room for a table or chest, and a hanging corner cupboard on a small landing expands a home's storage.

Right: Teddy bears and samplers guide the way to the upstairs suite. The extensive bear collection began 10 years ago, after the owner confided to a family member that he'd never had one as a child.

Above left: An island cottage with a no-frills layout includes this staircase that's open underneath. The banister was built by the owner.

Far left: A collection of canoes borders this third-floor studio.

Near left: A steep roof pitch causes the ceiling to sweep low in this loft bedroom.

PERSONAL SPACE

Right: The twig table and sofa in this third-floor family room were handcrafted.

Left: To create intimacy within a large space, decorate a corner as a room within a room. This private reading nook is actually part of an expansive living room.

For your own projects, on your own time, a quiet corner provides personal space where there's room for just one. Here you can spread out, stretch out, or camp out undisturbed, relying on cues from furniture arrangement to define your territory and signal your privacy. As shown here, a space to the side of a stairway is ideal for a reading table and chair, while a private corner is created by angling a daybed for an outdoor view.

Left: Filled with bright sun, a living room bay window is a perfect home for plants.

Above right: This window's decoy and other antique objects came from flea markets and lawn sales. The owners look for pieces with original paint, handcrafted design, and unusual details.

Below right: Family cowboy boots decorate the brick window ledge overlooking a side patio. Brick around all the windows in this home add texture and color.

A windowsill is such a simple thing—and so perfect for collections of handcrafts or baskets of blooms. From a bay window big enough to serve as the focal point of a room, to a sill so small that it's almost forgotten, these windows capture the light of the sun and direct it to the objects on display. ✳

Outdoor Views

From their breezy furniture to expansive views, porches invite family and friends to indulge in long conversations and lazy afternoons. By extending living space into the great outdoors, they blend the calm of their surroundings with all the comforts of home.

Preceding pages: A set of Adirondack chairs provide comfortable seating for this porch's pretty vantage point.

Left: This unique porch, one of the most photographed in Eureka Springs, Arkansas, is a fine example of traditional Victorian architecture.

Right: French doors open to capture this porch's garden effect and admit balmy Long Island breezes. The flowers include the garden's blooms and finds from a local florist.

Below: A renovation included building this porch, which has a view of the large acreage.

From across the street or down the road, a home's veranda says "welcome" to all who pass by. Set with chairs and flowers, it beckons visitors for a glass of iced tea and an afternoon of conversation. The

porches shown here make strong first impressions through interesting architecture, simple styling, and an abundance of blooms that turn a plain porch into a romantic retreat.

SUNNY SOLARIUMS

Right: Once used as a greenhouse, this conservatory is now referred to as the "sod room." The owners actually laid sod to give the inside room an outside feel.

Left: With glass on three sides and overhead, this kitchen eating area offers a sunny escape.

Below: This sunroom was built in stages. It began as a bark floor, then was covered by a roof. The owners added windows and eventually replaced the bark floor with used brick.

Offering both sun and shelter, solariums are perfect for daydreams and indulgences. Inviting the outdoors into the home, they add fresh-air appeal with scenic views, warm breezes, and delightful growing conditions for greenery of all kinds. The solariums pictured on these pages partner with nature, capturing the light, erasing the boundaries between indoors and out, and creating soothing places in the sun.

MEETING HALFWAY

An enclosed porch is an in-between place, halfway between the living space of the home and the recreation of the outdoors. It can be a spot to sleep overnight, with cool breezes drifting through screened windows, or to prepare bedding plants for their transfer to the garden. Generally more casual and easier to maintain than the rest of the home, porches allow for projects too messy for other rooms. And even in intemperate climates, they conveniently allow you to complete indoor/outdoor projects without worrying about the weather.

Right: A barn that has been transformed into a summer retreat for grandchildren includes this sleeping porch, where the children bunk overnight.

Left: This back porch is a workroom for handling a harvest of flowers, herbs, and vegetables.

Left: The wicker pieces on this sun porch were found at auctions, thrift shops, and estate sales. Because each is painted white and the same fabrics are used throughout, the furniture easily is grouped and regrouped into various combinations of settings.

Right: With a distinctive blue-sky ceiling and grass-green floor, this porch beckons family and friends for leisure-time enjoyment.

Below: A poplar-lined driveway leads to this sunny back porch, which provides an excellent view of the Cascade Mountains.

White wicker is as light as a breeze on a hot summer afternoon. While antique wicker is generally quite fragile, manufacturers today are designing wicker and wickerlike pieces that are durable and weather resistant. Dressed in coordinating patterns and colors, wicker pieces blend effortlessly with other furnishings, indoors and out.

RESTING PLACES

Right: The original copper-screened windows on this back porch were replaced with flat panes, and a cosmetic update produced a casual beach-house look with pale blue-and-white-striped cotton fabric on the sofa and window seats.

Left: The Gingerbread House, a bed and breakfast in Bay View, Michigan, has long welcomed guests to its quiet locale. The rockers on all the porches invite visitors to sit and enjoy the views.

Below: Leading directly into the living room, this front porch suggests an appreciation for the easy life.

When your goal is to sit back and watch the world go by, porches offer the perfect vantage point at different times of day. In fact, the direction a porch faces often determines when it will be most used. A western exposure will capture the harshest afternoon light (along with the most beautiful sunsets) and can be cooled with shady plantings. Porches that face east, north, and south offer more temperate views at all times of day.

RUSTIC APPEAL

Tucked away among the trees, these porches are rough around the edges, but they're soothing to the soul. Furnished with sturdy chairs and lounges of willow and bent twigs, they invite visitors to put their feet up and stretch out—the ultimate form of relaxation at a bed-and-breakfast inn or vacation cabin. The addition of flowers, cushions, and handcrafted accents softens the rustic exteriors.

Right: This log cabin was restored, transformed into a bed-and-breakfast inn, and expanded with the addition of a new guest room. Willow furniture on the porch echoes the building's rough exterior.

Left: Rustic bent-twig furniture fills a screened back porch on this vacation home in Michigan's northern reaches. The view includes a pond and abundant wildlife.

HOLDING COURT

Left: An oversized twig settee and chair purchased from a roadside stand are at home in their Santa Fe surroundings. The pillows and cushions echo the garden's rich hues.

Right: On this California patio, guests are invited to sample fine wines made from the owners' chardonnay grapes.

Below: Three pairs of French doors make easy access to this patio.

Like porches, patios expand a home's living space into the outdoors. When defined by walls, hedges, shrubs, or unique flooring, they become like courtyards—enchanting rooms that are most common and practical in temperate climates. Thanks to building materials that blend with their homes, the patios on these pages are natural extensions of gracious interior space.

Left: A sitting area outside a gracious old country house invites family and friends to relax.

Right: A pair of rocking chairs, cut flowers, floral fabrics, and an old braided rug bring simple Southern charm to this porch of an 1830s Georgia home.

Below: Furniture on this porch features knots, cracks, and burrows that add character to the pieces. The willow settee and side table are deliberately rustic.

Unlike the more gentrified indoor living space to which they're attached, porches can adopt a rambling, rough-and-tumble air that brings comfort from early morning into the late-night air. On these pages, a collection of cushioned furniture is drawn in a circle for old-time storytelling, while all-weather furniture and accents dress up rustic porches. ✳

Nature's Comforts

With imagination and an affection for country style, you can create rooms in the garden much as you would indoors. Any plot of land—no matter how large or small—can be "redecorated" with flowers and shrubs, allowing you to experiment with color and texture as you develop your garden design.

AT YOUR DOORSTEP

Preceding pages: Herbs spill over the borders, softening the formal design of this country garden.

Right: Easy-care flowers—pink, yarrow, salvia, crocosmia, Shasta daisy, linaria, and hollyhock—bloom just outside the door.

Left: Like a scene outside an English cottage, the over-grown look of this garden fits the style of the home.

Below: Clay pots and hanging baskets provide space for begonia, geranium, pansy, browallia, trailing verbena, and lobelia. The pots are moved during the day to catch the sun.

Homes surrounded by flower gardens are framed in freshness, with trailing vines and soft foliage helping to mask any sharp edges or plain exterior views. When those floral displays reside just beyond the threshold, you can enjoy them from inside as well as out, checking blooms from the kitchen window. As you plant a flower bed close to the home, mind the angles of the sun and requirements for proper drainage.

A Sense of Structure

Unbridled garden blooms look their best when defined by a simple structure. Whether it's a summerhouse covered with climbing plants or a wooden bridge softened by flowers, the straight lines of man-made structures provide contrast to a garden's natural exuberance.

Right: This old springhouse and its antique red clay roof tiles provide an ideal structure for climbing plants.

Above left: Sawdust paths and wooden bridges wind through masses of flowers, herbs, and grasses.

Far left: A gazebo with its own flowers is snuggled into these grounds.

Near left: Runner beans provide quick-growing and abundant greenery for an arbor while espaliered apple trees mature.

THE HERB GARDEN

Left: This herb garden follows a colonial-era design. The bountiful plants are used for vinegars, cooking, wreaths, and pressed flowers on writing cards.

Right: A crab apple tree pruned in a basket shape is at the heart of this fenced herb garden.

Below: Thyme, lemon balm, mint, pink hyssop, purple sage, and rue fill a circular herb garden. The pot at the base of the graceful arbor holds an unlikely but arresting planting of orange violas and **Ruby Bell cabbage.**

For centuries, herbs have captivated people with their sweet fragrances, delicate foliage, and pungent flavors. They've been ascribed magical and godlike powers (dill, for example, was said to ward off witches), are known to heal the sick, and today are loved primarily for the enchantment they lend to gardens and foods. The many varieties of herbs are ideal for small spaces, but the extent of their influence cannot be contained.

A Touch of Whimsy

Right: Inside a summerhouse, English ivy thrives along the rafters and twines around a cupola where a folk-art Adam and Eve are ensconced.

Left: An engaging spotted black rooster watches over red currant bushes. Nearby, a weathered deck chair nestled in a dappled clearing is the perfect spot for contemplation.

Below: Fanciful flea-market finds add personality to plantings.

The folk-art objects shown here are tucked among the flowers and foliage, offering gentle surprises for delighted wanderers. By introducing whimsical accessories into the garden, you can give a lighthearted personality to any outdoor space. In fact, mixing objects among the flowers can bring garden plantings into sharper relief, calling attention to shady places and secluded corners.

NATURAL RETREATS

With a decorating boost from nature, defined garden spaces can buffer city dwellings from urban sounds and cut down large yards into cozier places. You can create your own natural retreat by enclosing an area of the yard, then surrounding it with plantings abundant in fragrance and color.

Opposite: This patio vignette is framed by the tree, chairs, and doors. Ground cover, ornamental grass, and *Larix decidua Pendula* provide a background soft in both texture and color.

Above left: Shaded by a plumcot tree (a mix of plum and apricot), this table and Victorian chairs overlook a rose garden.

Left: The glass-top Chinese pedestal in this courtyard does double-duty as a bar when company arrives. The garden gates were made from garage doors salvaged from what now is the guesthouse.

THE WATER GARDEN

Left: The owners dug the garden pond and added the picket fence and arbor.

Above left: Rustic furniture invites people to linger near the small lily pond.

Above right: The sounds emanating from this tiered fountain shield the garden from noises outside and create a sense of privacy.

The soothing sound and perpetual motion of water add fascination to a garden setting. Like the focal point of a room, a water source simultaneously attracts attention and provides a backdrop for other garden features. Whether it flows in a large pond or a tucked-away fountain, water transforms a garden into a place for meditation. It invites a steady stream of wildlife to bathe and replenish, and it fills a landscape with sound and color. Powerful and reflective, animating and quieting, the water garden invites visitors to drink in its natural beauty.

BEYOND THE GARDEN GATE

Right: Clematis arches over the entry to a woodland garden. The gate was rescued from a nearby apartment complex that was undergoing demolition; the fence was salvaged from a dumpster. The choice of flowering vine was inspired by the work of famous English gardener Rosemary Verey.

Left: Pineapple garden ornaments from Italy, perched atop mortarless pedestals of brick, welcome visitors to this spring garden, shown in its fourth year of growth.

Below: This rose-laden arbor presides over beds of fibrous begonia, evening primrose, iris, and lamb's-ears.

A gate defines a garden entrance, just like a doorway defines a room, welcoming those outside to enter and enjoy what lies within. Cloaked in blooms and foliage, a gate provides a preview—a sneak peek at the glories of the garden. Yet it protects privacy, too, making visitors feel honored to be allowed through. In good fashion, the gates on these pages demonstrate that such first impressions are worth the effort—and that they can be achieved in a variety of natural ways.

Like rooms in a country house, gardens can be accessorized with one-of-a-kind objects that lend character and originality to their surroundings. As a focal point or a small surprise, accents add beauty, charm, and definition. They may be natural, like the firewood planters shown here, or elegantly crafted, like the cherubs or sculpted hand. By introducing accessories into the garden, you can expand an interest in collectibles and blend man-made beauty with that of Mother Nature.

Opposite: Lush ivy, potted Sunbelt Coral and Veronica Oglevee geraniums, and two smaller figures accent this garden statue. The columns were rescued from an old house that was being demolished.

Above left: Crooked, interesting shapes of firewood have been winnowed out to make excellent planters. The natural hollows are perfect for shade-loving plants, such as impatiens, wax begonias, and sedum.

Below left: This weathered "milagro" (in Spanish religious tradition, an item that is offered to commemorate a miracle) is hung among plants to symbolize the hand of the gardener.

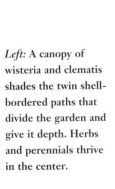

THE PATH LESS TRAVELED

Left: A canopy of wisteria and clematis shades the twin shell-bordered paths that divide the garden and give it depth. Herbs and perennials thrive in the center.

Above right: Parts of this garden's curving path feature bricks scavenged from demolished buildings. Clay chimney flues planted with herbs also define spaces.

Near right: Fuchsia, medicinal fern, old roses, and heirloom geranium plants crowd the stone and shell pathway that leads to a shaded back door.

Far right: A formal colonial garden brims with fragrant herbs and flowers, including antique English tea roses.

Paths lead us through life to mysterious places, to our next adventure, to the world of the unknown. In the garden, paths can give us direction and a sense of place. And when they connect us to abundant views of nature's comforts, they also give us reason to stop, rest, and enjoy the journey.

Style Notes
DECORATING WITH FLOWERS

While in the garden, flowers provide a colorful frame for a home's exterior. But once cut and brought inside, they become a focal point, providing a splash of brilliant color and a mix of textures. There are endless ways to arrange and use flowers throughout the home, ranging from a romantic canopy of dried blossoms to more traditional bouquets for mantels and side tables. For inspiration, these bountiful blooms combine cottage appeal and country colors to heighten the appreciation of any room in the house. ✳

Above left: Heirloom plants comprise a bouquet of stiking forms and textures. The flowers include prickly globe thistle and star-shaped tobacco flower.

Above right: A feather mattress and Log Cabin quilt are complemented by a bouquet of flowers.

Far left: A bouquet bursting with wildflowers brightens a cabin window.

Left: Ruffled poppies, hollyhocks, purple-blue larkspur, and bell-shaped campanula fit with the '40s-era fabric in this living room.

Below left: Old porch posts make the perfect addition to a bedroom—the bed sprouting into a four-poster with added height and sensual appeal. The stunning selection of dried flowers includes delphiniums, eucalyptus, calla lilies, baby's-breath, and roses.

Below right: Old-time favorites—delphinium, sweet pea, columbine, yarrow, and cosmos—are blended in this lush bouquet. With such a majestic mix, you don't have to be an expert at arranging flowers. The slightly haphazard appearance adds to the charm.

Cherished
Displays

Country collections honor the

beauty of everyday objects,

from well-loved toys to antique

pottery. Although there are no

hard-and-fast rules for

displaying your treasures, a few

guidelines—and a passion for

favorite things—will transform

a simple space into a showcase

for charming collectibles.

PURELY PRIMITIVE

Preceding pages: **Misfit animals find a new home on a circa-1830 Ohio jelly cupboard with its original apple-green paint.**

Opposite: **A free-standing mustard cupboard is lined with Shaker boxes, pails, and pantry boxes.**

Above left: **Covered pails, a hand-shaped cookie cutter, and a blue tin apple outfit a kitchen shelf.**

Below left: **Wooden kitchen utensils are just one of this owner's collections. A wall in the dining room is covered with cutting boards and breadboards.**

The appeal of primitives lies in their unadorned elegance—the patina of old wood, the simplicity of a hand-carved utensil, the splash of color on an old painted pail. By showcasing simplicity, the displays on these pages allow the rough beauty of the collectibles to shine.

PLAYFUL SURROUNDINGS

Opposite, above: Colorful majolica, vintage quilts, and antique prints and toys set an inviting scene.

Opposite, below: This couch and easy chair, found abandoned on roadsides, were transformed by fresh upholstery.

Above left: A diverse collection includes old benches painted in buttermilk colors, an outdoor trellis, and a polychrome parrot candleholder.

Below left: Metal cars and stuffed animals are scattered throughout this home, which also houses spillover from the owner's antique quilt shop.

Country collectibles can be absolutely delightful in their colorful, childlike appeal. By surrounding yourself with such treasures, you can create a mood that's both nostalgic and playful. As these rooms illustrate, interesting combinations result from spirited colors, varied textures, and completely unexpected finds.

STRIKING SIMILARITIES

Left: **Wooden bowls fill an antique cupboard.**

Below: **Perched above a weathered pine storage case, this assortment of aged birdcages adds rustic charm to a family room.**

One of the simplest ways to create a high-impact display is to group similar items. While a wooden bowl or antique stitchery might go unnoticed by itself, it carries weight and artistic appeal when surrounded by like objects. The displays on these pages let the items speak for themselves, complemented by only a few simple embellishments.

Above left: An assortment of stitcheries is enhanced by items that bring out the colors and styles of the needlework.

Below left: A favorite collection, displayed Shaker-style from a pegboard, includes children's chairs still bearing their original paint.

There's something magical about uneven numbers—and in decorating, three is company. Three vases, three hats, or a mix of three handmade items—a chair, a lamp, and a wall hanging—compose natural balance. Whether they're just alike or charmingly dissimilar, they create a symmetry that's pleasing to the eye.

Opposite: A row of three satin glass vases is as elementary as it can be, yet it adds elegance to the portrait in the background.

Above left: Striking in its simplicity, this grouping of cowboy hats hangs on a living room wall.

Below left: This arrangement of items, which were handcrafted by the owners, creates an artistic corner in a master bedroom.

SHELVING IT

Successful shelf arrangements are a matter of personal style, but a few simple guidelines can help you create the most pleasing displays. As illustrated on these pages, an eclectic mix of items adds interest through a variety of textures, combining glossy finishes and painted pottery with woven, glass, and wooden elements. Your display will have more depth if you choose items of different heights and set tall objects behind short ones. And to take collectibles to new levels, place items on lifts, such as wooden boxes, dishes, books, or flat-top baskets.

Opposite: Majolica, Limoges glass cherries, pottery bowls, and artwork fill an antique wall hutch.

Above, far left: In a guest bathroom, glazed minipots (on the middle shelf) made by the owner complement sundry artful objects.

Above, near left: An 1800s painted bucket bench overflows with a mix of contemporary and antique pottery. European cheese presses adorn the wall.

Below, left: Native American sweet-grass baskets and Staffordshire pottery stand in an old cupboard.

Above right: This windowsill's parade of folk art and flowers attests to the owner's passions.

Below right: A hanging pine cabinet and a clock outfitted with checks add character to a kitchen.

Above left: Vivid and eclectic collectibles add splashes of color to this kitchen's black-and-white color scheme.

Above right: Items from American history create a burst of red, white, and blue patriotism on a shelf above a bed.

Displaying collectibles is like telling a story. Depending on how you assemble the cast of characters and set the scene, you can tell a tale of childhood whimsies, unabashed patriotism, or nostalgia for a simpler time. In the displays on these pages, the individual items contribute to the impact of the whole. By choosing items that reflect your personal tastes or handiwork, you can turn an artful display of collectibles into the story of your life.

CLASSIC COMPOSITION

Right: Wood carvings are favorite collectibles in this well-balanced display.

Above left: In a keeping room, a dry sink bought at a flea market displays antique bowls.

Below, far left: These primitive antiques came from flea markets, estate sales, and junking excursions.

Below, near left: Artfully applied original paint attracted the owners to this rustic cupboard. The deep reds and greens blend perfectly with the decor. The unframed oil painting of apples on a red drape is one of many flea-market and tag-sale paintings that the owners have collected. $100 is the top price they'll pay.

Well-composed displays just *feel* right. Although often asymmetrical, they strike a soothing balance. On these pages, round plates soften the edges of a dry sink and shelf, bowls echo a painting that serves as a backdrop, and baskets fill space beneath a table to anchor the arrangement of items up above.

PERSONAL PASSION

Right: **Most of these colorful pieces of pottery came from the Alps region of France.**

Left: **Collections include beeswax and carved animals.**

Below: **Putz sheep made in Germany are among the owners' favorites. Another prize is the small Shaker box topping the stack on the upper shelf. A gift from a relative, it is dated 1770.**

Although it might be useful to be aware of the latest trends, the best collections are built from items *you* value the most. Surround yourself with treasures that represent memories from childhood, travels to your homeland, or special connections to family and friends, and you'll soon amass a collection that suits your personal style. ✳

Holiday Homes

During the holidays, country

comforts symbolize our most

cherished traditions. In the

treasures we unpack year

after year—the shiny antique

ornaments and the favorite

childhood trims—we're

reminded of our enduring

relationships and the warm

spirit of our homes.

Preceding pages: A fir tree is bedecked with contemporary and Victorian ornaments made of blown glass, fragile paper scraps, and shiny tinsel.

Left: This living room in a circa-1920 home reflects the owner's Scandinavian heritage. Blush-painted walls create a serene backdrop for the holidays.

Right: Antique lace covers this living room tea table and sofa, while wispy angel hair and garlands augment the romantic mood.

Below: This tree is hung with wide paper ribbon and wooden ornaments. The owner built the peak-roofed birdhouses.

During the holiday season, the main room of the house becomes a showplace for celebratory style. By dressing it in its annual best, you can enrich and complement the everyday ambience, yet still create a sense of comfort. On these pages, traditional greens shine against pastel backdrops, antique lace creates a veritable white Christmas, and rich colors invite visitors to enjoy a cozy conversation around the tree.

A HEARTY WELCOME

Right: In this dining room, the table is set for a Christmas brunch. A late-19th-century Log Cabin quilt made of wool challis drapes the old church pew.

Left: This keeping room showcases an early-1800s New England settle, late 1700s stool, a chair table bought from the home's former owner, and the owner's carved figures.

Below: This holiday table's centerpiece includes a pineapple—a colonial symbol of hospitality.

Traditionally, friends and family gather 'round the holiday table, celebrating the spirit of the season. The dining area offers ample opportunities for expressing holiday sentiments, from a traditional symbol of hospitality incorporated into a centerpiece, to touches of folk art or a table-side tree. Whether elegant or primitive, the dining area can create a celebration of its own, setting the mood for a yuletide feast.

A LONG WINTER'S NAP

Left: This little girl's bedroom is a study in family history. The baby dresses and tea set were her mother's, and the 1876 pegboard, rocking chair, and cedar chest were passed down from three generations of family members.

Right: Walls finished in white plaster accentuate the massive chestnut and pine beams left visible throughout this house. The bed was made by a decoy carver.

Below: Swags of greens and antique Santas soften the strong, straight lines in this 1700s home.

Just like the children in *The Night Before Christmas*, you and your family may dream of sugarplums when you bedeck your bedrooms for the holidays. On these pages, miniature trees convey a warm bedside manner, stuffed dolls and toys are dressed for the occasion, and boughs of greens and holly make fragrant swags to ensure sweet dreams. Like Santa himself, the magic of Christmas accents lends itself to lasting memories.

THE CHRISTMAS KITCHEN

Right: This kitchen retains its original function as well as its 1814 restored appearance. The owners cook meals on the hearth and make hand-dipped, beeswax candles here, which they frequently use for illumination.

Above left: These kitchen cabinets were designed to blend with the saltbox home's historical theme. Gingerbread cookies decorate the apple-cone tree, which was made by the owner.

Far left: A variety of tin cutters used in making sugar cookies rests atop a 19th-century fir cupboard.

Near left: Painted thumb-back 1830s Windsor chairs flank the Sheraton-style table, on which two jaunty snowmen reside. Other holiday decorations are made from natural materials, such as corn husk, wheat weavings, beeswax, and carved wood.

Decorated in Christmas finery, the kitchen is a festive spot in which to prepare the holiday fare. Cupboards, kitchen tables, and countertops are all ideal showcases for much-in-demand Christmas collectibles—particularly when the items include cookie cutters, an apple-cone tree, or other objects that support a home-baked or handmade theme.

Left: The owners transformed an ordinary bedroom by adding a pine floor, converting a closet into an alcove, and filling it with a spinning wheel and a reproduction cupboard.

Opposite: An unusual framed view of the bay at Naples rests on this bedroom's mantel. The owner painted the pair of planters and bleached the garland's pinecones white.

Below left: Original finishes adorn this keeping room's preserve cupboard and circa-1800 chair table.

Country holiday decor fits into every room of the house, filling ordinary spaces with festive charm. The mood can be reflected in a mantel swag of greens and pinecones, a well-placed poinsettia that enhances the warmth of old wood, or a spindly feather tree festooned with old-fashioned miniature ornaments.

SCENES FROM CHRISTMAS PAST

Left: Elegant paneling around the fireplace and boxed ceiling beams lend a sense of formality to this master bedroom. The table where Santa has left his pipe is an early shoe-foot hutch table.

Right: Miniature celluloid animals enliven a Christmas scene atop an antique German dower chest.

Below: Two well-loved teddy bears, an old clay pipe, a finger-joined trunk, and an antique sampler adorn the top of a blanket chest. Native cones, greens, and a clay Santa lend seasonal cheer.

Christmas can recall simpler times, when Santa's pipe and hat were left next to the fire, or when a favorite bear was a cherished companion. By grouping treasured Christmas collectibles or your most-loved toys from childhood, you can create vignettes from yesteryear as a statement of enduring holiday spirit.

FESTIVE ACCENTS

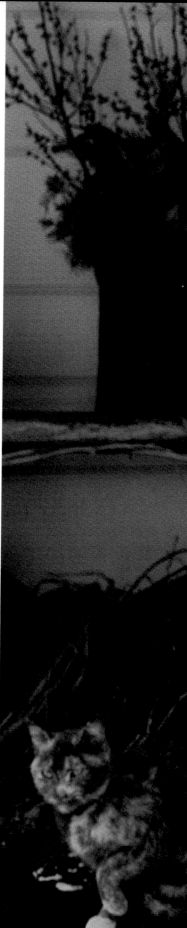

Winter holidays are magical. Every corner, every nook and cranny boasts treasures full of memories. The beauty and interest of seasonal decorating rests in these details, and in the personal and unique heirlooms that grace the home. Those cherished items may include the pinecone boughs that greet holiday guests, a cherished dollhouse from childhood that brightens a corner table, or a handmade Santa keeping watch from the mantel.

Right: Garlands of fresh greens are wrapped around front-porch posts.

Left: A handmade Santa and garland add cheer to 17th-century collectibles.

Below: This English dollhouse is dressed for the holidays. In this country, toys became popular gifts for children beginning in the mid-1800s.

TRADITIONAL TRIMS

Right: This tree is wrapped in grapevine and gold ribbon, and surrounded with collections of teddy bears, snowmen, and other toys and decorations.

Above left: A planter of topiaries serves as a backdrop for an old cast-iron toy Santa and his reindeer. A swag dangles gold-sprayed acorns and oak leaves.

Far left: A windowsill shows off a festive family of snowmen.

Near left: A feather tree is decorated with a collection of candles and Santas.

The holidays are a time for unabashed nostalgia and childlike joy.

Here, we offer inspiration with the whimsy of country collectibles.

Particularly noteworthy are ornaments and candle holders for the tree,

Santas, snowmen, nutcrackers, and Noah's arks.